A Ladybird Key Words Easy Reader

Some Great Men and Women

by W. MURRAY
with illustrations by
F. HUMPHRIS

Publishers: Wills & Hepworth Ltd. Loughborough
First published 1972   ©   Printed in England

King Alfred the Great of England
A.D. 849-900

King Alfred the Great was one of the first kings of England. He was a great and kind king. He did so much that was good for the people of England that he could have been called Alfred the Good.

In the time of Alfred the Great, not many men or women could read or write. Alfred could read and write well. He wanted his people to have schools where they could learn to read and write. While he was king, many people went to school for the first time in their lives.

Alfred was a brave man as well as a good one. While he was king, the Danes came in their boats to England and fought their way up the rivers. They wanted to live in England and make it their own country. Alfred and his people fought hard because they did not want to give up their country to the Danes.

0 7214 0306 9

The Ladybird Key Words Easy Readers are based on these commonly used words. Those used most often in the English language are introduced first — with other words of popular appeal to the learner. For example, the twelve most used words in English (a, and, he, I, in, is, it, of, that, the, to, was) which make up a quarter of all those the ordinary person reads and writes, are included in the 46 different words of Book 1.

Each book contains a list of the new words used. The gradual introduction of these words, frequent repetition and 'carry-over' from book to book, will ensure rapid learning.

The full-colour illustrations have been designed to create a desirable attitude towards learning, and to make the learner eager to read.

The information printed at the bottom of the coloured illustrations may be read aloud to the learner, to stimulate his interest further.

This series links with The Ladybird Key Words Reading Scheme. The author of both is W. Murray, an experienced headmaster, author and lecturer on the teaching of reading. W. Murray is co-author, with J. McNally, of ' Key Words to Literacy '—a teacher's book published by The Schoolmaster Publishing Co., Ltd., Derbyshire House, St. Chad's Street, London, W.C.1.

The Ladybird Key Words Easy Readers

These books are written on a controlled vocabulary and are graded in order of difficulty.

If the Teacher wishes, this series may be linked with the Ladybird Key Words Reading Scheme. Book One ("The Record Breakers") is about equal in reading difficulty to the third level of the Reading Scheme (i.e. Books 3a, 3b, 3c), Book Two ("Danger Men") with the fourth stage (4a, 4b, 4c) and so on.

Older non-readers may use these Ladybird Key Words Easy Readers as books for learning to read. Other children will also be attracted because of their interest and appeal.

King Alfred discussing the building of a new Saxon church.

Marco Polo of Venice
1254-1324

Today, people can travel to all parts of the world. They can travel from country to country on railways or in cars, aeroplanes, ships or hovercraft. Some men have even been to the moon and back.

When Marco Polo lived, there were no railways, cars or aeroplanes, and only very small ships. There were no maps like the ones we use today, and it was hard for a traveller to find his way even on a journey through his own country. People in the west did not know how people in the east lived.

Marco Polo and his father made a very long journey from west to east and back again to the west. They went from Venice in Italy to China and back to Italy.

They were many years on this long journey and sometimes were in great danger while on the way.

Marco Polo and his father passing through dangerous, mountainous country on their way to China.

Marco Polo's great journey

You can find Venice on your map of the world. You can see what a long way it is from China. On their journey east to China, Marco Polo and his father went through many countries and across many rivers and high mountains before they reached China.

At that time the great Kubla Khan was Emperor of China. Kubla Khan liked Marco Polo, who worked for the Emperor and his people and made many long journeys across China for them. Marco Polo and his father were in China for sixteen years. They worked hard and became rich.

The time came when they wanted to go back to Venice. Kubla Khan said they could go and they made the long journey back to Italy.

Marco Polo could read books and write well, so he made maps of the countries he went through and made a book about his long journey.

After their long journey from Venice, Marco Polo and his father meet Kubla Khan, the Emperor of China.

William Caxton and the printing press
1422-1491

There were no printing presses in England before the time of William Caxton. In those days, the people used to write books by hand with pen and ink. It took a long time to write a book with pen and ink, so there were not many books and not many people could learn to read and write.

William Caxton first saw a printing press in Germany when he was on a journey through that country. He went to Germany again to learn all he could about printing. When he came back to England, William Caxton made a printing press like those he saw in Germany.

Caxton was helped in his work by three kings of England. They helped him with money as he was not a rich man.

Many more men, women and children learned to read and write because of the thousands of books which William Caxton could print on his printing presses.

William Caxton shows a friend the pages of the first book ever printed in England.

Christopher Columbus
1450-1506

In the days when Christopher Columbus lived, most people said that the world was flat. Christopher Columbus said that it was round, and today we know that it is round and not flat.

For some years Christopher Columbus had made maps for a living and had learned all he could about ships and the sea. Columbus wanted to get ships of his own and sail them to the west and on round the world to the east. He learned of the journey to the east made by Marco Polo and his father, and how these travellers became rich in the east.

Christopher Columbus was not a rich man. He asked the king of his own country, and the kings of other countries, for money to build some ships, but they would not give him any money.

At last someone helped him to get three ships and the men to sail in them. Then Christopher Columbus was able to sail west across the Atlantic Ocean.

Christopher Columbus finds other people unwilling to believe that the world is round and that he could sail west and reach India.

The West Indies

When the three small ships sailed across the Atlantic Ocean and away to the west, many people thought they would never come back again. Some thought that as the earth was flat, the ships would sail to the end and fall off. Some thought that the ships would get lost or sink to the bottom of the sea.

The journey that Christopher Columbus made was a long and hard one. Christopher Columbus was brave and so were many of the men in his crew. But there were some in the crew who were afraid. There were no maps to help them and they were afraid they would be lost. They thought that any day could be their last.

As time went by, more and more of the crew became afraid. They wanted Columbus to go back but he would not.

At last they came to an island. Christopher Columbus thought it was India. It was not India but one of the islands we now call the West Indies. We call them the West Indies because this is what Christopher Columbus thought they were.

Christopher Columbus sails towards the West Indies.

Francis Drake
1542-1595

After Christopher Columbus sailed to the West Indies, people went to live in those and other countries west of the Atlantic Ocean. They called these countries the 'New World'. Spain was a country of the 'Old World' which became rich with the gold found in the New World.

Ships went from Spain to the New World to take this gold back to Spain. Francis Drake sailed with ships from England to take this gold from them. Many times Francis Drake led his crews and fought against those of Spain.

At one time Francis Drake sailed round the world. Four of the ships he led were lost on the way and in the end only one came back to England. He was the first Englishman to sail right round the world.

When England and Spain were at war, Drake fought against Spain. The King of Spain sent many ships and men to make war against England. Drake led the English ships against them and won.

One of Sir Francis Drake's small ships attacks a large galleon of the Spanish Armada.

Walter Raleigh
1552-1618

England became a great country in the time of Queen Elizabeth I, thanks to men like Francis Drake. Another great man of the time was Walter Raleigh.

Walter Raleigh was a brave man who had many adventures. He fought in the war between England and Spain. He was a great traveller and wrote books about his journeys to the New World. Three times he sailed west across the Atlantic Ocean to find more countries and gold in the New World.

After one of his journeys, he came back with potatoes and tobacco. There were no potatoes or tobacco in England before the time of Walter Raleigh. Now potatoes and tobacco are used in many countries. We can thank Walter Raleigh for potatoes but we know now that tobacco is not good for us.

Elizabeth liked Walter Raleigh and he became a rich man while she was Queen. When Elizabeth was dead, the new King of England did not like Walter Raleigh and he had his head cut off.

Queen Elizabeth being presented with potatoes brought from South America by Walter Raleigh.

William Shakespeare, playwright
1564-1616

William Shakespeare was a great playwright who lived in Stratford-upon-Avon and in London in the time of Queen Elizabeth I.

Most people say that William Shakespeare was the greatest playwright this country has ever had. Some say that he was the greatest playwright the world has ever known. His plays are known to people everywhere.

William Shakespeare lived in Stratford-upon-Avon as a boy and went to school there. In Stratford-upon-Avon we can see the school he went to, and the house where he lived as a boy. It was in London that he wrote many of his greatest plays. Queen Elizabeth liked to see the plays he wrote.

After many years in London, William Shakespeare went back to end his days in Stratford-upon-Avon. He was a rich man then and could live in a large house. We can see this house, which is near his school.

William Shakespeare reads one of his plays to some of his friends.

Captain James Cook
1728-1779

Captain James Cook was an explorer. He was one of England's greatest explorers. There are many books about him and the journeys he made.

Captain Cook lived in the days of sailing ships. In those days there were many parts of the world which had never been explored. There were no maps of the countries and oceans of those parts.

Captain Cook could make very good maps. He sailed to the other side of the world and made maps of the seas and oceans he sailed across, and the countries he found.

Men who sailed the seas in those days had many adventures, and many ships were lost at sea. When Captain Cook's ship was near Australia it hit a rock. At first the crew thought that it would sink and were very afraid, but it did not sink and they sailed on to Australia.

When they reached Australia, Captain Cook put up the English flag. Now Australia has its own flag.

Captain Cook and his crew land in Australia.

More about Captain Cook

Captain Cook was a very brave man and the crews he had were brave too. His crews liked him because he looked after them well. Not many men were lost on his journeys round the world.

The King of England thanked Captain Cook for all that Cook had done for his country. The king liked to hear him talk about the countries he had been to, and the seas and oceans he had sailed across. He knew how much Captain Cook liked to go to sea, so he gave him more work to do.

At that time, men thought that there must be a way to sail from the North Pacific Ocean to the North Atlantic Ocean. Captain Cook sailed to the North Pacific Ocean to find this way, but he came to a sea of ice. His ship could not get through the ice and he had to sail back into the South Pacific Ocean.

In the south he then found some islands which had never before been found.

A sea of ice prevents Captain Cook from sailing further north in the Pacific.

Admiral Horatio Nelson
1758-1805

Nelson went into the navy as a boy. It was a very hard life in the navy then. Nelson was always small and not very strong, but he was brave, worked hard and loved ships. He became a captain and then, after some years, an admiral. He was the most famous admiral England has ever had.

At that time, England was at war with France. There were many battles at sea. Nelson fought against France for years, and England won the war. He was hurt many times in his battles at sea.

Nelson loved England and always did his duty. Before he fought his last and most famous battle against France, the flags of his ship read:

"England expects that every man will do his duty".

He led his ships into battle and won the battle but lost his own life.

Horatio Nelson, a great English admiral.

Elizabeth Fry
1780-1845

People in prison have a very hard life. No-one likes to be in prison. But today, being in prison is not as bad as it was in the time of Elizabeth Fry.

In those days, men and women in prison had a very bad time. Today, we would not let animals live the way prisoners lived then. Elizabeth Fry saw how bad the prisons were and that even children went to prison in those days. When a mother went to prison, her children had to go with her if there was no-one to look after them. Elizabeth Fry fought to make sure that those children could go to school in prison.

This good woman did all she could to make life better for all prisoners. She wrote a book about what she saw.

Most people thought that Elizabeth Fry was right in what she said, and things did get better. Her book was read in other countries and she was asked to go to some of them to talk about her work.

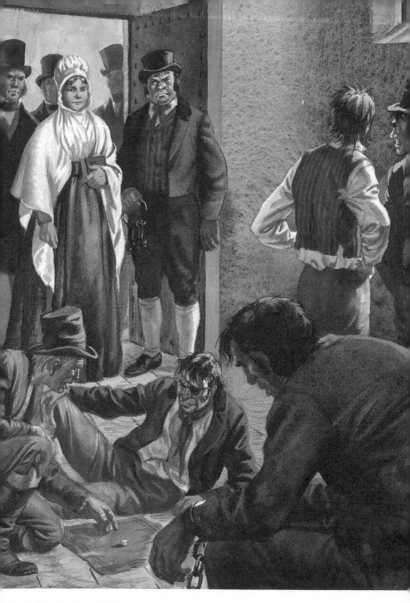

Elizabeth Fry visiting a prison.

Louis Braille
1809-1852

Louis Braille lived in France. When he was a little boy only three years old, he became blind.

Louis went to a school for blind children. Before long, he wanted to learn to read books and music. In those days no blind people could read. No-one had thought of any way to help them to learn to read.

Louis Braille was very clever. He was so clever that he thought of a way to help the blind to read. He used raised dots on the paper, not printed letters. Someone who was blind could touch the raised dots on the paper and be sure which letter it was. In this clever way, blind people can soon read books and music.

When books or music are printed with these raised dots, they are said to be printed in Braille—because of Louis Braille. Books like these help blind people all over the world.

Louis Braille finds a way to help blind people to read.

David Livingstone, missionary and explorer
1813-1873

David Livingstone's great wish as a boy was to be a missionary. He became a doctor first and then a missionary. He was a great missionary and one of the greatest explorers any country has had.

It was his wish to help people that made David Livingstone go to Africa. Men knew little about Africa before he went there. For many years Livingstone helped men, women and children there, not only as a missionary but as a doctor.

Doctor Livingstone was in Africa most of his life. He was exploring much of the time, and went on very long journeys to parts where only Africans had been before.

On one journey he found the Victoria Falls. The Victoria Falls are famous now. Doctor Livingstone named them 'Victoria Falls' after Victoria, the Queen of England at that time.

David Livingstone reaches the falls which he named after Queen Victoria.

Florence Nightingale
1820-1910

Florence Nightingale lived in the time of Queen Victoria. She was rich and did not have to work for a living. But she thought it her duty to help others. She liked to help in hospitals.

In those days, many hospitals were dirty. They had too many beds to a room and not enough nurses. Some hospitals were not as well run as they should have been, and people died who should not have died.

When England was at war, wounded men were not looked after as well as they should have been. There were no women nurses and many wounded men died.

Florence Nightingale was the first woman nurse to go to war. After a time, other women nurses went to help her. They found the wounded in dirty rooms with no beds and not enough to eat or drink. They looked after the wounded and many of these men lived because of the way they were looked after.

Queen Victoria wrote to Florence Nightingale to thank her and her nurses for the way they had helped the wounded. A famous school for nurses, in London, was named after Florence Nightingale.

Florence Nightingale visiting the wounded in a military hospital.

Louis Pasteur, the great French chemist
1822-1895

Louis Pasteur was a great French chemist. He found that there were bacteria in the air and on things all around us. No-one knew about bacteria before this French chemist made his discoveries.

Bacteria are so very small that they can be seen only when they are magnified.

Some bacteria are good for us; some other kinds of bacteria make us ill. Some can make us very ill and even kill us.

Louis Pasteur also discovered how to kill some of the bacteria which make us ill.

Because of the discoveries of this clever French chemist, some of our milk is 'pasteurised' to kill the bacteria which could make us ill.

Louis Pasteur at work in his laboratory.

Joseph Lister
1827-1912

Joseph Lister was a famous English surgeon. He lived at a time when a great many people died in hospital after operations. Joseph Lister found out why.

Louis Pasteur had discovered that there were bacteria in the air and on things all around us.

Joseph Lister found that these germs could get into the blood, through a wound or cut, and poison it. He found a way to stop these germs getting into the blood. He used antiseptics—which killed the germs before they could get into the blood.

All surgeons in hospitals now use antiseptics. Nowadays people do not get blood poisoning after operations in hospitals.

There are antiseptics of one kind or another in most homes today.

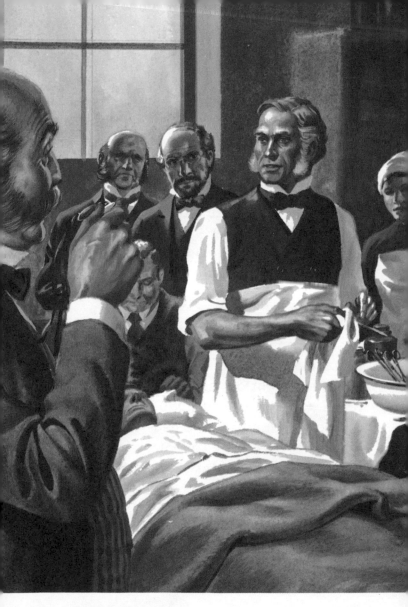

Joseph Lister sterilizes his instruments to kill the germs which cause blood-poisoning.

Thomas Edison, inventor
1847-1931

Thomas Edison was an American inventor. An inventor is a man who makes something that no-one has thought of before. Edison was so clever that today many of his inventions are in use all over the world.

One of his most useful inventions was electric light. Before the time of Thomas Edison, many people used oil or gas for light. Now people in most countries use electric light.

Thomas Edison was also the inventor of the gramophone. Another inventor thought of the telephone, but Thomas Edison worked on that invention and helped to bring the telephone into everyday use. Many of Edison's inventions helped the Americans when at war. The people of his country thought he was the greatest American of his time.

When we use electric light, the gramophone or the telephone, we should sometimes think of this famous American and what he did for us all.

Thomas Edison, inventor of the electric light bulb, demonstrates his invention to his friends.

Madame Curie
1867-1934

Madame Curie was a famous scientist. Her husband was a scientist, too, and helped her in her great work of discovering radium. Radium gives off rays which we cannot see. These rays can go through things that we cannot see through. With rays like these, a doctor can see inside us.

The rays from radium can be used to cure people who are ill, but they are also dangerous. Madame Curie and her husband became ill because of these rays. At first, they did not know that the rays could be dangerous.

One day, Madame Curie's husband was killed in the street, but this brave woman went on with her great work.

In the First World War, this great scientist helped in hospitals. The rays given off by the radium she had discovered, were used to help cure many men and women.

Marie and Paul Curie return to their laboratory at night and see radium glowing in the darkness.

Albert Schweitzer
1875-1965

Albert Schweitzer was very clever in many ways. He was so clever that he could have been a rich man in his own country of Germany.

However, Albert Schweitzer became a doctor and then left Germany to live and work with poor people in Africa. Many of them had no hospitals, no doctors and no nurses.

One of Albert Schweitzer's great loves was music. He raised money by playing music, and with this money he built his own hospital in Africa. This was in a part of Africa which was then French. He lived and worked in that hot country for many years, helping to cure the poor people who were ill.

At times, this good doctor left Africa to go to Germany to raise money for his work. Nothing could stop him going back to Africa. Other people who knew of his life's work in Africa went there to help him.

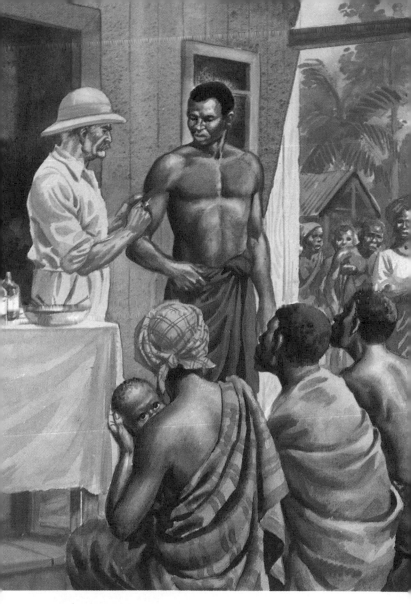

Albert Schweitzer treating the sick in Africa.

Winston Churchill
1874-1965

Winston Churchill was a great Englishman and a great leader.

When England was at war against Germany, many people thought the Germans would win. Winston Churchill never thought like that. He was afraid of nothing. When things looked black, he would make great speeches. These speeches made the 'man in the street' sure that the war could—and would—be won.

In the end, the war against Germany was won. His speeches became famous.

Winston Churchill liked to write. He wrote many books. Some of these are about England—the country he loved so much.

This great Englishman had an American mother. Because of this, and because he was such a great leader, he was liked by many Americans.

Winston Churchill touring bomb-damaged London during the Second World War.

Helen Keller
1880-1968

When Helen Keller was a baby, she was very ill and then became blind, deaf and dumb. She went to many hospitals, but no doctor or surgeon could cure her. It was thought then that anyone who was blind, deaf and dumb could never learn to talk or read and write.

Helen Keller was very clever and she did learn to talk, and to read and write. First, she learned to talk. Then she learned to read Braille by touch. After a time she could write like other people. She wrote letters and books, and learned to read and play music. She travelled from America to countries all over the world.

Helen Keller loved life. She said life was an adventure. Most of all she loved children, animals, and flowers.

Many people who are not blind, deaf or dumb cannot do some of the things Helen Keller did.

Helen Keller, the blind, deaf and dumb girl who learned to speak, read and write.

Write out these 20 questions and the answers

1. Which king was the first to help his people to read and write? *See page 4*

2. Where did Marco Polo end his first journey from Italy? *See pages 6 and 8*

3. Who made the first printing press in England? *See page 10*

4. Who sailed to the west to find the countries of the east? *See page 12*

5. Why are the West Indies so named? *See page 14*

6. Name the first man from England to sail round the world. *See page 16*

7. Who came back to this country with the first tobacco and potatoes? *See page 18*

8. Which great playwright lived at Stratford-upon-Avon? *See page 20*

9. Who first put up the English flag in Australia? *See page 22*

10. Who was the most famous admiral England has had? *See page 26*